Democracy at Risk:
The Dangers of Project 2025

Democracy at Risk:
The Dangers of Project 2025

J. E. Fowlers

Table of Contents

Introduction

Project 2025 is a significant and ambitious initiative spearheaded by the Heritage Foundation, a prominent conservative think tank in the United States. The project aims to reshape various aspects of American governance and policy, consolidating power within the executive branch and implementing sweeping changes across multiple federal agencies.

People are talking about this initiative for a good reason: it outlines a set of policy proposals that could be implemented if certain candidates or parties gain power. And if that happens, we'll no doubt see major changes to how our government and public services work, affecting everything from education and healthcare to our rights and freedoms. Each of us needs to understand these changes because they could impact our daily lives, reduce protections and support for vulnerable communities, and concentrate power in ways that might undermine democracy. By learning about Project 2025, we can better protect our rights, ensure fair policies, and engage in actions that support a just and equitable society. That's what this book is all about.

Let's start from the beginning. The origins of Project 2025 can be traced back to a growing movement among conservative leaders and organizations seeking to strengthen executive authority and reduce what they perceive as bureaucratic inefficiencies within the federal government. The Heritage Foundation, with its extensive network and influence, emerged as a key architect and advocate for this initiative, rallying support from various conservative groups, political figures, and donors.

Key Players

The Heritage Foundation: Founded in 1973, the Heritage Foundation is a think tank known for its influence on conservative policy-making. It has been instrumental in developing and promoting the vision and objectives of Project 2025.

Conservative Political Leaders: Various elected officials and influential political figures have endorsed and supported Project 2025, viewing it as a means to advance conservative principles and policy goals.

Donors and Financial Backers: A network of wealthy individuals and organizations has provided the financial resources necessary to drive the project forward, ensuring that it has the funding needed to influence policy and public opinion.

Federal Agencies and Departments: Project 2025 targets several federal agencies for restructuring or elimination, with the aim of centralizing power and streamlining government operations. Key agencies in the crosshairs include the Department of Education, the Environmental Protection Agency, and others.

Grassroots Conservative Groups: These organizations have mobilized their members and supporters to advocate for Project 2025, engaging in public awareness campaigns and lobbying efforts to build broad-based support.

By understanding the origins and key players behind Project 2025, we can better grasp its motivations and potential impacts. Now, let's explore how Project 2025 could reshape American democracy and affect various aspects of society.

Objectives and Vision

Project 2025 aims to fundamentally reshape the structure and function of the U.S. government, driven by a vision of a more centralized and streamlined executive branch. The key objectives and vision of Project 2025 include:

Centralization of Power

The project seeks to consolidate authority within the executive branch, reducing the influence of other branches of government and independent federal agencies. By doing so, it aims to create a more cohesive and efficient governance structure where decision-making is faster and more aligned with the executive's agenda.

Restructuring Federal Agencies

A major component of Project 2025 is the overhaul of various federal agencies. This involves either significant restructuring or outright elimination of agencies deemed unnecessary or counterproductive. The goal is to reduce bureaucracy, cut down on regulatory burdens, and streamline government operations.

Enhancing Executive Authority

The project envisions a substantial increase in the executive branch's power and reach. This includes granting the President and executive officials more control over policy implementation and regulatory frameworks, thereby ensuring that their vision and directives are more directly realized.

Promoting Conservative Values

At its core, Project 2025 is driven by conservative principles. It seeks to promote policies that align with these values, such as reducing government intervention in the economy, enhancing national security, and preserving traditional social norms. The project aims to use the enhanced executive power to further these goals more effectively.

Reducing Federal Spending

A key objective is to lower federal expenditures by cutting down on wasteful spending. This includes reducing funding for programs and agencies that do not align with the project's vision or that are seen as inefficient. The savings from these cuts are intended to be redirected toward other priorities, such as defense or tax cuts.

Streamlining Regulations

Project 2025 intends to drastically cut back on federal regulations, particularly those that are perceived as hindering business and economic growth. By simplifying the regulatory landscape, the project aims to create a more business-friendly environment, encouraging innovation and investment.

Empowering State and Local Governments

The project also envisions devolving more power to state and local governments. By reducing federal oversight and giving more autonomy to states, it seeks to encourage more localized and tailored governance solutions that better address the unique needs of different regions.

Ensuring National Security

A significant part of the vision includes strengthening national security measures. This involves not only military enhancements but also stricter immigration policies and a more robust homeland security framework to protect the nation from various threats.

The overarching vision of Project 2025 is to create a more efficient, streamlined, and conservative federal government that can act decisively and effectively in pursuing its policy goals. By centralizing power and reducing bureaucratic constraints, the project aims to transform the American governmental landscape in ways that reflect its core values and objectives.

Why Are People Worried About It Now?

Concerns about Project 2025 have been mounting for several reasons, primarily centered around its potential to fundamentally alter the democratic landscape of the United States. With the 2024 presidential election, there's a possibility that Project 2025 could soon become a reality. Here are some of the key reasons why people are worried:

Threats to Democratic Institutions

Many fear that the centralization of power within the executive branch could undermine the system of checks and balances that is foundational to American democracy. Concentrating authority could make other branches of government, such as the legislative and judicial branches, less effective in holding the executive accountable.

Erosion of Civil Liberties

Project 2025's plans include measures that could significantly impact individual freedoms and rights. For example, increased surveillance and restrictions on freedom of speech and assembly are potential outcomes that worry civil liberties advocates. The rollback of reproductive rights and civil rights initiatives are also seen as major threats to personal freedoms.

Impact on Education

The proposal to dismantle the Department of Education and redirect funds could lead to significant disparities in educational quality and access. Critics argue that this could exacerbate existing inequalities and undermine the public education system, making it harder for students from disadvantaged backgrounds to succeed.

Economic Inequality

Some view Project 2025's emphasis on deregulation and free-market policies as a pathway to increased economic inequality. By reducing social safety nets and welfare programs, the project could disproportionately affect vulnerable populations, leaving them without essential support and widening the gap between the rich and the poor.

Judicial Independence

The potential restructuring of federal agencies and changes in the judiciary are seen as threats to judicial independence. If the executive branch gains too much influence over the courts, it could lead to biased rulings that favor the administration's agenda, undermining the impartiality that is crucial for a fair legal system.

Environmental Concerns

Deregulation efforts that aim to reduce oversight by agencies like the Environmental Protection Agency could lead to weaker environmental protections. This raises alarms about the potential for increased pollution, degradation of natural resources, and a lack of accountability for environmental harm.

Historical Parallels

This isn't the first time something like this has happened in our world. There are historical examples of similar centralization of power leading to authoritarian regimes. The potential for Project 2025 to follow this trajectory is a significant concern for those who value democratic governance and fear the rise of autocratic rule.

Impact on Minority Rights

The targeting of diversity, equity, and inclusion (DEI) initiatives and the redefinition of discrimination are seen as direct threats to the progress made in racial and gender equality. The rollback of protections and support for marginalized communities could reverse decades of civil rights advancements.

Media Suppression

Plans to control and suppress media that is critical of the government raise serious concerns about freedom of the press. A free and independent media is essential for transparency and accountability, and any moves to undermine it could severely impact democratic discourse.

Mobilization of Resistance

The awareness of these potential threats has led to increased mobilization among advocacy groups, legal challenges, and public awareness campaigns. The urgency of these efforts underscores the widespread concern about the direction in which Project 2025 could take the country.

In summary, the worry about Project 2025 stems from its potential to radically change the fundamental structures and principles of American democracy, impacting civil liberties, economic equality, environmental protections, and the independence of various institutions. The broad scope and significant implications of these proposed changes have raised alarms among a diverse range of stakeholders.

The Importance of Understanding Project 2025

Project 2025 is not just another political initiative; it represents a comprehensive effort to reshape the American government and society. Understanding this project is crucial for several reasons, particularly because of its potential impacts on democracy and society.

Project 2025 proposes significant changes to the structure of the U.S. government. By centralizing power within the executive branch, it aims to streamline decision-making processes. However, this shift could undermine the balance of power among the three branches of government, which is a cornerstone of American democracy. This centralization might lead to reduced oversight and accountability, giving the executive branch unprecedented control.

America's system of checks and balances is designed to prevent any one branch of government from becoming too powerful. Project 2025's emphasis on enhancing executive authority poses a threat to this system. If the executive branch gains more control over federal agencies and the judiciary, it could bypass the legislative process and enact policies unilaterally, weakening the role of Congress and the courts.

One of the most significant concerns is the potential erosion of civil liberties. Project 2025 includes measures that could increase government surveillance and reduce privacy rights. Additionally, proposed restrictions on freedom of speech and assembly could stifle dissent and limit public discourse. These changes could lead to a society where individual freedoms are significantly curtailed.

Furthermore, by targeting the Department of Education for restructuring or elimination, Project 2025 could drastically alter the landscape of American public education. This could lead to reduced funding for schools, greater inequality in educational opportunities, and a shift towards privatization. The long-term effects could be a less equitable education system that fails to serve all students effectively.

Project 2025's economic policies, which emphasize deregulation and free-market principles, could exacerbate economic inequality. While these policies might benefit large corporations and wealthy individuals, they could reduce social safety nets and welfare programs that support vulnerable populations. This could lead to increased poverty and a widening gap between the rich and the poor.

The project's potential influence over the judiciary is another major concern. By appointing judges who align with its ideology, Project 2025 could shape the judicial landscape for decades. This could result in a judiciary that is less independent and more inclined to uphold the executive branch's agenda, undermining the principle of impartial justice.

Deregulation efforts proposed by Project 2025 could also weaken environmental protections. Reducing the oversight of agencies like the Environmental Protection Agency (EPA) might lead to increased pollution and environmental degradation. This could have long-term consequences for public health and the planet's sustainability.

Project 2025's policies could also bring about significant social and cultural changes. For instance, its stance on reproductive rights and civil rights could roll back decades of progress in gender equality and racial justice. This could lead to increased discrimination and social tension, affecting the cohesion and inclusivity of American society.

Finally, changes in domestic policy could also affect the U.S.'s position on the global stage. Project 2025's emphasis on national security and stricter immigration policies might strain relationships with other countries and affect international cooperation. This could have broader implications for global stability and the U.S.'s role in world affairs.

Understanding Project 2025 is essential because its potential impacts are far-reaching and profound. By comprehending the scope and implications of this initiative, citizens can better engage in informed discussions, advocate for or against specific policies, and participate actively in the democratic process. Recognizing the potential consequences helps ensure that any changes to the government and society align with the values of democracy, justice, and equality.

Chapter 1: The Blueprint for Authoritarianism

Project 2025 seeks to fundamentally transform the structure and functioning of the U.S. government by achieving three primary goals: centralizing power within the executive branch, restructuring federal agencies, and empowering executive authority. Each of these goals is designed to streamline governance, reduce bureaucratic inefficiencies, and ensure that the executive branch can implement its agenda more effectively.

However, these changes also raise significant concerns about the erosion of democratic principles, the weakening of checks and balances, and the potential for authoritarian practices. Understanding these goals in detail can help us appreciate the massive impact that Project 2025 could have on American democracy and society. This analysis will explore the specific strategies proposed for achieving these goals, the rationale behind them, and the potential risks and consequences associated with their implementation.

Centralization of Power

One of Project 2025's primary goals is to centralize power within the executive branch of the U.S. government. The purpose of this centralization is to streamline decision-making, reduce bureaucratic inefficiencies, and ensure that the executive can implement its agenda more effectively. However, this shift raises significant concerns about the balance of power that is fundamental to American democracy.

Key Aspects:

- **Reducing Congressional Oversight:** By consolidating power, the executive branch may bypass the traditional checks and balances provided by Congress. This could lead to executive actions being implemented without the rigorous scrutiny and debate typically involved in the legislative process.

- **Increasing Executive Control Over Agencies:** Centralizing power allows the President and executive officials to exert greater control over federal agencies, ensuring that these agencies align with the administration's goals and policies.

- **Potential for Authoritarianism:** The concentration of power within the executive branch can pave the way for authoritarian practices, where the executive operates with minimal accountability and oversight.

Restructuring Federal Agencies

Project 2025 proposes a comprehensive restructuring of federal agencies to reduce bureaucracy, enhance efficiency, and align agency functions with the project's overall goals. This restructuring involves significant changes to how agencies operate, their funding, and their regulatory authority.

Key Aspects:

- **Elimination and Merging of Agencies:** Some agencies may be eliminated or merged to streamline government functions. This can lead to cost savings but may also reduce the government's ability to address specific issues effectively.

- **Redirection of Funds:** Funds from eliminated or downsized agencies would be redirected to other areas deemed more critical by the executive branch. This reallocation could impact public services and programs previously managed by these agencies.

- **Regulatory Overhaul:** The restructuring effort includes a significant reduction in regulations that are viewed as burdensome.

While this may benefit businesses, it could also reduce protections for consumers, the environment, and public health.

Empowering Executive Authority

Empowering the executive authority is a central tenet of Project 2025. The project plans to expand the powers of the President and executive officials to ensure that their directives are implemented swiftly and without obstruction. This empowerment is seen as essential for achieving the project's broader goals.

Key Aspects:

- **Executive Orders and Directives:** The use of executive orders and directives would be increased to bypass legislative gridlock. This allows the President to implement policies quickly without needing congressional approval.

- **Appointments and Personnel Changes:** Empowering the executive includes appointing loyalists to key positions within the federal government. These appointments ensure that the executive's policies are enforced consistently across all levels of government.

- **Legal and Constitutional Challenges:** Expanding executive authority often leads to legal and constitutional challenges, as opponents argue that such actions violate the separation of powers. These challenges can create significant political and legal battles that shape the future of American governance.

By analyzing these goals in detail, we can better understand the far-reaching implications of Project 2025. The centralization of power, restructuring of federal agencies, and empowerment of executive authority are aimed at creating a more efficient and responsive government. However, they also pose risks to democratic principles, accountability, and the balance of power that are fundamental to the American political system.

Historical Parallels with Authoritarian Regimes

To understand the potential dangers of Project 2025, it is essential to examine historical parallels with authoritarian regimes. Throughout history, there have been numerous instances where similar efforts to centralize power, restructure government institutions, and enhance executive authority have led to the erosion of democratic norms and the rise of authoritarian rule. These historical examples provide valuable insights into the potential consequences of Project 2025.

1. Nazi Germany:

- **Consolidation of Power:** Adolf Hitler's rise to power involved the systematic dismantling of democratic institutions and the centralization of power within the executive branch. The Enabling Act of 1933 gave Hitler the authority to enact laws without parliamentary consent, effectively rendering the Reichstag powerless.

- **Restructuring Institutions:** The Nazi regime restructured various government agencies to align them with its ideological goals, purging officials who were not loyal to the party and consolidating control over all aspects of governance.

- **Empowering Executive Authority:** Hitler's unchecked executive authority allowed him to implement policies swiftly, leading to widespread human rights abuses and the establishment of a totalitarian state.

2. Soviet Union:

- **Centralization of Power:** Joseph Stalin centralized power within the Communist Party, eliminating political opposition and consolidating authority within the executive branch. This centralization was achieved through purges, show trials, and the suppression of dissent.

- **Restructuring Government Agencies:** The Soviet regime restructured government agencies to ensure they served the party's interests, creating a highly centralized and bureaucratic state apparatus.

- **Empowering Executive Authority:** Stalin's absolute control over the state apparatus enabled him to implement policies such as collectivization and the Great Terror, resulting in widespread repression and the loss of millions of lives.

3. China under Mao Zedong:

- **Consolidation of Power:** Mao Zedong's leadership of the Chinese Communist Party involved the centralization of power and the elimination of political rivals. The Cultural Revolution further consolidated Mao's authority, leading to significant political and social upheaval.

- **Restructuring Institutions:** Mao's regime restructured various institutions to align them with communist ideology, often through violent means. The Cultural Revolution targeted intellectuals, government officials, and party members perceived as disloyal.

- **Empowering Executive Authority:** Mao's unchecked authority allowed him to implement radical policies such as the Great Leap Forward, which led to economic disaster and widespread famine.

4. Venezuela under Hugo Chávez:

- **Centralization of Power:** Hugo Chávez's government centralized power within the executive branch, undermining democratic institutions and reducing the independence of the judiciary and the legislature.

- **Restructuring Institutions:** Chávez restructured government institutions to ensure loyalty to his regime, including purging the military and appointing loyalists to key positions.

- **Empowering Executive Authority:** Chávez used executive decrees to bypass the legislative process, implementing policies that eroded civil liberties and led to economic instability.

5. Hungary under Viktor Orbán:

- **Centralization of Power:** Viktor Orbán's government has been characterized by the centralization of power within the executive branch, undermining the independence of the judiciary and reducing the effectiveness of parliamentary oversight.

- **Restructuring Institutions**: Orbán's regime has restructured various government institutions to ensure they align with his political agenda, including changes to the electoral system that favor his party.

- **Empowering Executive Authority:** Orbán's expanded executive authority has allowed him to implement policies that restrict media freedom and civil liberties, leading to concerns about democratic backsliding.

These historical parallels make it clear that the centralization of power, restructuring of government institutions, and enhancement of executive authority can lead to the erosion of democratic norms and the rise of authoritarianism. Vigilance is extremely important—we need to safeguard democratic institutions against similar threats posed by Project 2025.

Potential Consequences for Checks and Balances

One of the most significant concerns regarding Project 2025 is its potential to disrupt the delicate system of checks and balances that underpins American democracy. This system is designed to ensure that no single branch of government becomes too powerful, providing a framework for mutual oversight and accountability. The centralization of power and restructuring of federal agencies proposed by Project 2025 could have far-reaching consequences for this balance. Here are some of the potential impacts:

Diminished Legislative Oversight

Reduced Congressional Power

By consolidating authority within the executive branch, Project 2025 could significantly diminish the role of Congress in overseeing the executive. This would make it harder for legislators to hold the President and executive agencies accountable for their actions.

Bypassing the Legislative Process

The increased use of executive orders and directives to implement policy changes can bypass the traditional legislative process, undermining the role of Congress in crafting and debating laws.

Weakened Judicial Independence

Influence Over the Judiciary

Enhancing executive authority often involves appointing judges who align with the administration's ideology. This can lead to a judiciary that is less independent and more inclined to uphold the executive's agenda, compromising its ability to act as a check on executive power.

Threats to Judicial Review

The restructuring of agencies and changes to administrative procedures could limit the scope of judicial review, making it harder for courts to scrutinize and challenge executive actions.

Erosion of Federalism

Centralization of Authority

Project 2025's emphasis on centralizing power can erode the principles of federalism by reducing the autonomy of state and local governments. This centralization can lead to a more uniform but less responsive governance structure, where local needs and preferences are overlooked in favor of national directives.

Preemption of State Laws

Increased executive authority might also involve preempting state laws that conflict with federal policies, undermining the ability of states to govern independently and address their unique circumstances.

Curtailment of Agency Independence

Politicization of Agencies

Restructuring federal agencies to align with the executive's goals can lead to the politicization of what were once independent bodies. This undermines their ability to provide unbiased oversight and implement policies based on expertise rather than political considerations.

Reduced Regulatory Oversight

The push to streamline and reduce regulations can weaken the ability of agencies to act as a check on corporate and governmental misconduct, potentially leading to increased corruption and reduced accountability.

Concentration of Executive Power

Authoritarian Tendencies

The consolidation of power within the executive branch increases the risk of authoritarian tendencies. A powerful executive with minimal checks can implement policies unilaterally, reducing transparency and accountability.

Executive Overreach

Without robust checks and balances, there is a greater risk of executive overreach, where the President and executive officials exercise powers beyond their constitutional limits. This can lead to the abuse of power and undermine the rule of law.

Impact on Democratic Norms

Erosion of Democratic Traditions

The gradual erosion of checks and balances can weaken democratic norms and traditions, making it more difficult to restore them once they have been undermined. This can lead to a long-term decline in democratic governance and public trust in institutions.

Public Disillusionment

As checks and balances erode, public confidence in the fairness and accountability of the government may diminish. This can lead to increased political polarization, cynicism, and disengagement from the democratic process.

Given the potential consequences for checks and balances, Project 2025 poses significant risks to the foundational principles of American democracy. Safeguarding these principles requires vigilance, active engagement, and a commitment to maintaining the balance of power among the branches of government.

Chapter 2: Dismantling the Department of Education

Project 2025 includes a comprehensive plan to radically alter the landscape of American public education. One of its most controversial proposals is the elimination of the Department of Education and the redirection of its funds. This plan aims to decentralize educational governance, reduce federal oversight, and promote alternatives to the traditional public education system. In this chapter, we look at details on exactly how it intends to do so.

Elimination and Redirection of Funds

1. Abolishing the Department

Proponents of Project 2025 argue that the Department of Education represents unnecessary federal overreach into a domain that should be managed by state and local governments. They believe that eliminating the Department will reduce bureaucracy and allow for more localized control over education.

The plan involves phasing out the Department of Education over several years. This would be achieved through legislation that gradually reduces its funding and transfers its responsibilities to other federal agencies or directly to state governments.

2. Redirecting Funds

The funds previously allocated to the Department of Education would be redirected to various initiatives that align with Project 2025's vision. This includes increasing funding for school choice programs, such as vouchers and charter schools, which proponents believe will create competition and improve educational outcomes.

A significant portion of the redirected funds would go directly to states, allowing them to tailor their educational systems to better meet the needs of their populations. This approach is intended to foster innovation and flexibility at the state level.

Impact on K-12 and Higher Education

K-12 Education

The redirection of funds towards vouchers and charter schools is expected to significantly expand school choice options for parents and students. Advocates argue that this will lead to better educational outcomes by fostering competition and innovation among schools.

Critics of the plan argue that expanding school choice could exacerbate educational inequities. Public schools, which serve the majority of students, may suffer from reduced funding and resources, leading to a decline in the quality of education for students who remain in the traditional public school system.

Without federal oversight, there are concerns about the consistency and quality of education across different states and districts. States may adopt varying standards, which could lead to disparities in educational quality and outcomes.

Higher Education

The elimination of the Department of Education could lead to significant reductions in federal funding for higher education, including grants and student loans. This could make it more difficult for students to afford college, particularly those from low-income backgrounds.

The plan may also involve reducing federal regulations that govern higher education institutions. While this could decrease administrative burdens, it could also lead to a lack of oversight and accountability in areas such as student loans, accreditation, and for-profit colleges.

Reduced federal involvement in higher education could impact access and affordability. Without federal grants and loans, students may have to rely more on private funding sources, which could limit opportunities for those who cannot secure sufficient financial support.

Project 2025's plan for the Department of Education has far-reaching implications for both K-12 and higher education. While proponents argue that these changes will lead to greater efficiency and localized control, critics warn of potential negative impacts on educational equity, access, and quality. Careful consideration of the potential consequences and trade-offs involved in such a significant restructuring of the American education system is essential.

Consequences for Educational Equity and Civil Rights

The proposed elimination of the Department of Education and the redirection of its funds as outlined in Project 2025 could have profound consequences for educational equity and civil rights. Here are the key potential impacts:

Increased Inequality in Education:

- **Resource Disparities:** Redirecting funds to school choice initiatives like vouchers and charter schools could widen the gap between well-funded and underfunded schools. Public schools, which rely heavily on federal funding, may experience budget shortfalls, leading to larger class sizes, fewer resources, and diminished educational quality, particularly in low-income and rural areas.

- **Access to Quality Education:** Wealthier families might benefit more from increased school choice options, as they often have the means to supplement vouchers or pay for additional costs associated with charter and private schools. Meanwhile, disadvantaged students could be left with fewer high-quality educational opportunities.

Impact on Civil Rights Protections:

- **Title IX and Anti-Discrimination Enforcement:** The Department of Education plays a crucial role in enforcing civil rights laws, including Title IX, which prohibits gender discrimination in federally funded education programs. Eliminating the Department could weaken enforcement mechanisms, leading to increased discrimination and reduced protections for students based on gender, race, disability, and other factors.

- **Special Education Services:** Federal oversight ensures that students with disabilities receive appropriate services and accommodations under the Individuals with Disabilities Education Act (IDEA). Without the Department of Education, there is a risk that these students might not receive the support they need, exacerbating educational disparities for students with disabilities.

Equity in Funding and Resources:

- **Variability Across States:** The decentralization of educational governance could lead to significant variability in funding and resources across states and districts. States with less capacity or willingness to invest in education may fall behind, creating a patchwork system where educational quality and access are highly dependent on geographic location.

- **Federal Grants and Programs:** The elimination of federal grants and programs that target underserved communities, such as Title I funding for low-income schools, could lead to increased inequities. These programs are designed to level the playing field and provide additional support to students who need it the most.

Impact on Minority and Marginalized Communities:

- **Racial and Socioeconomic Disparities**: Project 2025's proposed changes could disproportionately affect minority and low-income students. These communities often rely more heavily on federal support and protections to ensure access to quality education and equitable treatment.

- **Civil Rights Investigations:** The Department of Education's Office for Civil Rights conducts investigations into complaints of discrimination in schools. Without this oversight, incidents of discrimination may go unchecked, and affected students might have fewer avenues for recourse and justice.

Long-Term Societal Implications:

- **Economic Mobility:** Education is a critical factor in economic mobility and reducing poverty. Increased educational inequality could have long-term effects on economic opportunities and social mobility for disadvantaged students, perpetuating cycles of poverty and limiting the overall economic growth and stability of the country.

- **Social Cohesion:** A less equitable education system could lead to greater social stratification and reduced social cohesion. Disparities in educational outcomes can contribute to broader societal divisions and tensions, undermining the social fabric of the nation.

In summary, the elimination of the Department of Education and the redirection of its funds as proposed by Project 2025 could significantly impact educational equity and civil rights. The potential increase in resource disparities, weakening of civil rights protections, and heightened inequities in funding and access could have far-reaching consequences for students, particularly those from marginalized and disadvantaged communities.

Long-term Effects on American Public Education

The long-term effects of dismantling the Department of Education, as proposed by Project 2025, could reshape the landscape of American public education in profound ways. Here are some of the key potential impacts:

Increased Educational Disparities

- **Widening Achievement Gaps:** The redirection of funds towards school choice initiatives could exacerbate existing achievement gaps. Wealthier families might benefit from increased options, while students in underfunded public schools could face declining educational quality.

- **Regional Inequalities:** Without federal oversight to ensure equitable distribution of resources, disparities between affluent and low-income regions are likely to grow. States with less funding and fewer resources may struggle to provide quality education, leading to significant regional variations in educational outcomes.

Decline in Public School Funding

- **Budget Shortfalls:** As funds are redirected to vouchers and charter schools, public schools could experience significant budget shortfalls. This reduction in funding could lead to cutbacks in essential programs, staff layoffs, and deterioration of school facilities.

- **Impact on Programs and Services:** Reduced funding could force public schools to cut important programs, including arts, sports, and extracurricular activities, which are crucial for holistic student development. Support services such as counseling, special education, and advanced placement courses might also be negatively impacted.

Erosion of Educational Standards

- **Inconsistent Quality:** The absence of a centralized body to enforce educational standards could result in inconsistent quality of education across states and districts. States may adopt varying curriculums, assessments, and graduation requirements, leading to disparities in student preparedness for higher education and the workforce.

- **Loss of Accountability:** Without federal oversight, there may be less accountability for educational outcomes. Schools might not be held to the same standards of performance and equity, potentially lowering the overall quality of education.

Challenges for Teachers

- **Job Security and Salaries:** Public school teachers could face job insecurity and stagnant or reduced salaries due to budget cuts and shifting priorities. This could lead to higher turnover rates and difficulties in attracting and retaining qualified educators.

- **Professional Development:** Funding for teacher training and professional development may be reduced, limiting opportunities for educators to improve their skills and stay updated with best practices in teaching.

Impact on Higher Education

- **Reduced Access and Affordability:** Federal grants and student loans are crucial for making higher education accessible and affordable for many students. The elimination of the Department of Education could lead to decreased funding for these programs, making college less accessible to low-income and middle-class students.

- **Variability in Institutional Quality:** Without federal accreditation and oversight, there may be greater variability in the quality of higher education institutions. This could lead to the proliferation of subpar institutions, making it harder for students to navigate their educational choices and ensuring value for their investment.

Long-term Economic Implications

- **Workforce Readiness:** A decline in the quality of education could result in a workforce that is less prepared for the demands of the modern economy. This could impact the country's competitiveness on a global scale and hinder economic growth.

- **Social Mobility:** Education is a key driver of social mobility. Increased disparities in educational quality and access could entrench socioeconomic divides, making it harder for individuals from disadvantaged backgrounds to improve their economic standing.

Impact on Civic Engagement

- **Civic Literacy:** Education plays a crucial role in fostering civic literacy and engagement. A less equitable education system could lead to lower levels of civic knowledge and participation, undermining the health of American democracy.

- **Social Cohesion:** The public education system serves as a unifying force in society, bringing together students from diverse backgrounds. Increased segregation by income and race due to school choice initiatives could reduce social cohesion and increase societal divisions.

As we have seen, the long-term effects of dismantling the Department of Education and redirecting its funds, as proposed by Project 2025, could lead to significant challenges for American public education. These changes may increase educational disparities, reduce funding and resources for public schools, erode educational standards, and impact the broader economy and society. Understanding these potential consequences is essential for evaluating the overall impact of Project 2025 on the future of American education.

Chapter 3: Reproductive Rights Under Siege

Project 2025 takes a firm stance on reproductive rights, aiming to impose significant restrictions on abortion and access to contraceptives. This approach is driven by a conservative ideology that seeks to limit reproductive choices in the name of preserving traditional values and protecting what it defines as the rights of the unborn. Here's a detailed look at the project's stance and its potential legal and social implications:

Restrictions on Abortion and Contraceptives

Limiting Access to Abortion

Project 2025 proposes enacting stringent legal restrictions on abortion, potentially including near-total bans, mandatory waiting periods, and additional barriers such as mandatory counseling sessions designed to dissuade women from proceeding with an abortion.

The project also includes measures to defund organizations that provide or advocate for abortion services, such as Planned Parenthood. This would reduce the availability of abortion services, especially for low-income individuals who rely on these providers for affordable care.

Increasing regulatory requirements for clinics that provide abortion services, such as stricter building codes and hospital admitting privileges for doctors, could force many clinics to close, further limiting access.

Restricting Access to Contraceptives

Project 2025 aims to roll back mandates that require health insurance plans to cover contraceptives, making it more difficult for women to afford birth control. This could lead to a decrease in contraceptive use and an increase in unintended pregnancies.

By restricting federal funding for contraceptive services, particularly through Title X and other public health programs, access to affordable contraception could be severely curtailed, disproportionately affecting low-income individuals.

The project may include provisions that protect the rights of pharmacists and other healthcare providers to refuse to dispense contraceptives based on religious or moral objections, further limiting access.

Legal and Social Implications

Legal Battles and Constitutional Challenges

The restrictions proposed by Project 2025 are likely to lead to numerous legal battles, potentially culminating in significant Supreme Court rulings. These cases could challenge established precedents such as Roe v. Wade and Planned Parenthood v. Casey, which currently protect the right to access abortion.

States that support Project 2025's stance on reproductive rights may pass laws that align with its objectives, leading to a patchwork of regulations across the country. This could create significant disparities in reproductive health access based on geographic location.

Impact on Women's Health and Autonomy

Restricting access to safe and legal abortions could lead to an increase in unsafe, illegal procedures, posing serious health risks to women. Additionally, reduced access to contraceptives could lead to higher rates of unintended pregnancies and associated health complications.

- **Economic and Social Consequences:** Women who are unable to access abortion services may face economic and social hardships, including the inability to pursue education or career opportunities. This could perpetuate cycles of poverty and limit women's autonomy and decision-making power regarding their own lives.

Social Polarization and Activism

The stringent restrictions proposed by Project 2025 are likely to galvanize both pro-choice and pro-life activists, leading to increased social polarization and public demonstrations. This activism could manifest in widespread protests, legal advocacy, and intensified public discourse on reproductive rights.

Local communities, particularly those with limited healthcare infrastructure, may experience heightened tensions and conflicts as residents navigate the implications of reduced reproductive health services.

Global Perception and Influence

The stance taken by Project 2025 could influence global perceptions of the United States' commitment to women's rights and reproductive health. It may also embolden similar movements in other countries, potentially leading to a broader rollback of reproductive rights internationally.

International human rights organizations may raise concerns about the impact of Project 2025 on women's rights, potentially leading to criticism and calls for the U.S. to uphold its commitments to gender equality and health care access.

Case Studies of Past Reproductive Rights Rollbacks

The Hyde Amendment

Examining historical case studies of reproductive rights rollbacks can provide valuable insights into the potential consequences of Project 2025. One significant example is the impact of the Hyde Amendment in the United States, first passed in 1976. This legislative provision barred the use of federal funds for abortions, except in cases of rape, incest, or danger to the life of the mother. The Hyde Amendment disproportionately affected low-income women who relied on Medicaid for their healthcare needs, severely limiting their access to safe and legal abortions. Over the years, this restriction has highlighted the profound impact that funding limitations can have on reproductive rights and access to healthcare services.

The Global Gag Rule

Another illustrative case is the global gag rule, formally known as the Mexico City Policy. First implemented by President Ronald Reagan in 1984, this policy prohibits foreign non-governmental organizations (NGOs) that receive U.S. federal funding from performing or promoting abortions as a method of family planning. The global gag rule has been repeatedly enacted and rescinded depending on the administration in power, creating a seesaw effect that disrupts the provision of reproductive health services worldwide. When in place, the policy has led to the closure of clinics, reduced access to contraceptives, and increased rates of unsafe abortions, particularly in developing countries.

Poland's Near-Total Abortion Ban

In recent years, Poland has become a notable example of reproductive rights rollbacks in Europe. In 2020, the Polish Constitutional Tribunal ruled that abortions due to fetal defects were unconstitutional, effectively imposing a near-total ban on abortions in the country. This decision sparked widespread protests and international condemnation, as it significantly restricted women's access to safe abortions. The case of Poland demonstrates how legal changes can swiftly and severely curtail reproductive rights, leading to public unrest and highlighting the fragility of such rights even in democracies.

Texas Senate Bill 8 (SB8)

Additionally, the situation in Texas with the passage of Senate Bill 8 (SB8) in 2021 underscores the potential for state-level restrictions to challenge federal protections for reproductive rights. SB8 effectively banned most abortions after about six weeks of pregnancy and deputized private citizens to enforce the law through civil lawsuits against anyone aiding or abetting an abortion. This innovative enforcement mechanism has created significant legal and practical challenges for abortion providers and has led to a chilling effect on access to reproductive healthcare in the state. The Texas law illustrates how creative legislative approaches can circumvent established legal protections and set precedents for other states to follow.

These case studies collectively show the various ways reproductive rights have been rolled back—whether through funding cuts, policy shifts, legal rulings, or state legislation. They highlight the need for constant vigilance and advocacy to protect these rights. The potential consequences are significant and far-reaching when these rights are undermined, making it crucial to mobilize efforts to protect reproductive freedoms in the future.

Potential Impacts on Women's Health and Autonomy

The restrictions proposed by Project 2025 could have significant and far-reaching impacts on women's health and autonomy. Limiting access to abortion and contraceptives not only affects individual health outcomes but also has broader social and economic consequences.

Health Risks: Restricting access to safe and legal abortions can lead to an increase in unsafe, illegal procedures. Women who cannot access professional medical care may resort to dangerous methods to terminate unwanted pregnancies, resulting in severe health complications, infections, or even death. Additionally, reduced access to contraceptives can lead to higher rates of unintended pregnancies, which may result in more women seeking unsafe abortions or experiencing complications from pregnancies they are unprepared for.

Economic and Social Consequences: Women who are unable to access abortion services often face economic hardships. Unplanned pregnancies can derail educational and career plans, limiting women's opportunities for economic advancement and perpetuating cycles of poverty. The financial burden of raising a child without adequate resources can strain families and communities, leading to long-term socio-economic disadvantages. Furthermore, limited access to contraceptives can exacerbate these issues by increasing the likelihood of unintended pregnancies.

Autonomy and Decision-Making Power: Access to reproductive health services is crucial for women's autonomy and the ability to make informed decisions about their own bodies and lives. Restrictive policies undermine this autonomy by limiting the choices available to women, forcing them to carry pregnancies to term against their will. This loss of control over reproductive decisions can have profound psychological and emotional impacts, affecting women's overall well-being and sense of agency.

Impact on Minority and Low-Income Women: The effects of reproductive rights rollbacks are often felt most acutely by minority and low-income women. These groups are more likely to rely on public health services and may have fewer resources to seek alternative care when access to reproductive health services is restricted. As a result, they face greater risks of negative health outcomes and economic instability. The compounding effects of discrimination and economic hardship can further marginalize these women, exacerbating existing inequalities.

Long-Term Health Implications: Consistent access to comprehensive reproductive health care, including contraception and abortion services, is essential for maintaining women's health. Limitations on these services can lead to higher rates of maternal mortality and morbidity, as well as increased instances of chronic health conditions related to pregnancy and childbirth. The long-term health implications of restricted reproductive rights can have lasting effects on women's overall health and quality of life.

The potential impacts of Project 2025's proposed restrictions on women's health and autonomy are extensive. By limiting access to safe abortions and contraceptives, these policies can lead to increased health risks, economic and social hardships, and a significant erosion of women's rights and freedoms. When we understand these potential consequences, we can more effectively advocate for policies that protect and promote women's health and autonomy.

Chapter 4: Rolling Back Civil Rights

Project 2025 proposes significant changes to civil rights policies, focusing on targeting diversity, equity, and inclusion (DEI) initiatives and redefining discrimination in ways that could undermine decades of progress.

Targeting DEI Initiatives

Project 2025 aims to dismantle or significantly alter diversity, equity, and inclusion initiatives across various sectors, including education, government, and private industry. Proponents argue that these initiatives promote reverse discrimination and unfair advantages based on race and gender rather than merit. They claim that eliminating or scaling back DEI programs will foster a more meritocratic society.

Reduction in DEI Programs

The plan includes cutting funding for DEI programs in educational institutions, government agencies, and workplaces. This could result in the elimination of scholarships, training programs, and policies designed to promote diversity and support underrepresented groups.

Impact on Hiring and Promotion Practices

By targeting DEI initiatives, Project 2025 seeks to revise hiring and promotion practices that consider race, gender, and other identity factors. This could lead to a reduction in affirmative action policies and a return to more traditional hiring criteria, which may disadvantage minority candidates who have historically benefited from these programs.

Redefining Discrimination

Project 2025 also seeks to redefine what constitutes discrimination, shifting the focus from systemic issues to individual acts of bias. This approach aims to narrow the scope of civil rights protections and reduce the regulatory burden on businesses and institutions.

Narrowing Legal Definitions

The project proposes narrowing the legal definitions of discrimination to focus primarily on explicit, intentional acts of bias rather than systemic or institutional practices. This could make it more challenging for individuals to prove discrimination in courts and reduce the number of cases that qualify for legal protection.

Impact on Protected Classes

Redefining discrimination in this way could weaken protections for various groups, including racial minorities, women, LGBTQ+ individuals, and people with disabilities. By shifting the emphasis away from systemic discrimination, Project 2025 could undermine efforts to address broader social and institutional biases that affect these communities.

Limiting Enforcement Powers

The project also includes measures to limit the enforcement powers of agencies like the Equal Employment Opportunity Commission (EEOC). By reducing the scope and authority of these agencies, Project 2025 aims to decrease the regulatory and compliance burdens on businesses, potentially at the expense of protecting civil rights.

Project 2025's approach to civil rights, which includes targeting DEI initiatives and redefining discrimination, represents a significant shift from current policies. These changes could lead to the dismantling of programs designed to promote diversity and equity and make it harder to address systemic discrimination. The project's implications are far-reaching, affecting not just policy but the very fabric of American society and its commitment to justice and equality for all.

Implications for Racial and Gender Equality

Project 2025's proposed changes to civil rights policies carry significant implications for racial and gender equality. By targeting diversity, equity, and inclusion (DEI) initiatives and redefining what constitutes discrimination, the project risks reversing decades of progress in promoting equal opportunities and combating systemic biases.

Reduced Opportunities for Marginalized Groups: By dismantling DEI programs, Project 2025 could significantly reduce opportunities for marginalized groups in education, employment, and other sectors. These initiatives have played a critical role in providing access to resources, support, and opportunities for individuals who have historically faced discrimination and exclusion. Without these programs, racial minorities and women might find it more challenging to achieve equitable outcomes.

Increased Workplace Discrimination: The project's emphasis on narrowing the definitions of discrimination to focus on explicit acts of bias rather than systemic issues could lead to an increase in workplace discrimination. Employees who face subtle or systemic forms of discrimination may find it more difficult to seek redress, resulting in a less inclusive and supportive work environment for racial minorities and women.

Educational Inequities: Cutting funding for DEI initiatives in educational institutions could exacerbate existing inequities in education. Programs designed to support underrepresented students, such as scholarships, mentorships, and support services, are crucial for leveling the playing field. Without these resources, students from marginalized backgrounds may struggle to access the same quality of education and opportunities as their peers.

Erosion of Affirmative Action: Project 2025's approach could lead to the weakening or elimination of affirmative action policies. These policies have been instrumental in addressing historical injustices and ensuring that racial and gender diversity is considered in hiring and admissions processes. Without affirmative action, the progress made in diversifying workplaces and educational institutions could stall or reverse, perpetuating inequalities.

Legal and Social Setbacks: Redefining discrimination to exclude systemic issues could result in fewer legal protections for those experiencing racial and gender discrimination. This shift could embolden discriminatory practices, as businesses and institutions may feel less compelled to address biases that are not explicitly covered by narrower legal definitions.

Widening Socioeconomic Gaps: The rollback of DEI initiatives and broader civil rights protections could widen socioeconomic gaps between racial and gender groups. Economic disparities, already a significant issue, could deepen as marginalized groups lose access to critical support systems that help mitigate the effects of discrimination and provide pathways to economic mobility.

It goes without saying that the implications of Project 2025 for racial and gender equality are profound and concerning. The potential dismantling of DEI programs and the narrowing of discrimination definitions threaten to undermine the progress made towards achieving equal opportunities and combating systemic biases. These changes could lead to increased discrimination, reduced opportunities, and wider socioeconomic gaps, reversing the strides made in promoting a more inclusive and equitable society.

Analysis of Potential Legal Battles and Societal Backlash

The implementation of Project 2025's civil rights policies is likely to ignite significant legal battles and provoke substantial societal backlash. These conflicts will play a crucial role in shaping the future of civil rights in America.

Legal Battles

Constitutional Challenges

The narrowing of discrimination definitions and the rollback of DEI initiatives will almost certainly face challenges in the courts. Advocates for civil rights will argue that these changes violate constitutional protections, such as the Equal Protection Clause of the Fourteenth Amendment, which guarantees equal treatment under the law. Lawsuits may be filed to block or reverse policies that are seen as discriminatory or as weakening protections for marginalized groups.

Federal vs. State Jurisdiction

As federal oversight is reduced, states may implement their own DEI programs and civil rights protections, leading to a patchwork of laws across the country. This could result in conflicts between state and federal authorities, with states challenging the federal government's efforts to curtail their initiatives. These disputes could escalate to the Supreme Court, where rulings will set important precedents for the balance of power between state and federal governments in protecting civil rights.

Employment and Education Lawsuits

Companies and educational institutions that previously adopted DEI initiatives to comply with federal guidelines might face legal uncertainty. Lawsuits could arise from individuals claiming that the rollback of these programs leads to discriminatory practices or creates hostile environments. Additionally, organizations may face legal challenges for continuing DEI practices that the new policies seek to dismantle.

Societal Backlash

Public Protests and Advocacy

The rollback of civil rights protections and DEI initiatives is likely to provoke widespread protests and activism. Civil rights organizations, community groups, and concerned citizens will mobilize to defend existing protections and demand the restoration of DEI programs. Public demonstrations, marches, and social media campaigns could gain momentum, putting pressure on policymakers and influencing public opinion.

Corporate Responses

Many corporations have embraced DEI initiatives as part of their commitment to social responsibility and equitable practices. The new policies may force companies to choose between complying with federal mandates and maintaining their DEI programs. Some corporations may publicly oppose the rollbacks, using their influence to advocate for the continuation of diversity and inclusion efforts.

Impact on Public Trust

The perception that civil rights are being eroded could lead to a decline in public trust in government institutions. Communities that feel targeted by these policies may experience increased alienation and frustration, leading to greater societal divisions. Efforts to reduce discrimination protections could exacerbate existing tensions and contribute to a more polarized society.

Media Coverage and Cultural Shifts

Extensive media coverage of the legal battles and societal backlash will shape public discourse on civil rights. Debates over the merits and consequences of Project 2025's policies will likely dominate news cycles, influencing cultural attitudes toward diversity, equity, and inclusion. This heightened visibility could lead to a cultural shift, with increased awareness and advocacy for civil rights protections.

Electoral Implications

The controversy surrounding Project 2025's civil rights policies could impact electoral politics. Candidates and political parties will likely take strong stances for or against the proposed changes, using them as key issues in their campaigns. The public's reaction to these policies could influence election outcomes, potentially leading to shifts in political power at the local, state, and national levels.

The proposed changes to civil rights policies under Project 2025 are expected to generate significant legal and societal responses. Legal battles will test the constitutionality of these changes, while societal backlash will manifest through protests, corporate actions, and shifts in public opinion. For good reason, the broader impact of Project 2025 on American civil rights and social cohesion is of significant concern.

Chapter 5: The End of Criminal Justice Reform

Project 2025 includes a comprehensive approach to criminal justice, characterized by a strong opposition to reform efforts and an emphasis on law and order. This stance reflects a desire to revert to more traditional, punitive approaches to crime and punishment, countering recent trends toward criminal justice reform.

Opposition to Reform Efforts

Project 2025 aims to roll back many of the progressive policies that have been implemented in recent years to address systemic issues within the criminal justice system. These policies include efforts to reduce mass incarceration, eliminate cash bail, decriminalize certain offenses, and implement restorative justice practices. The project views these reforms as overly lenient and believes they undermine public safety.

One of the primary targets of Project 2025 is the elimination of mandatory minimum sentencing laws, which have been a significant focus of criminal justice reform advocates. The project supports reinstating these laws to ensure consistent and severe punishment for crimes, particularly drug-related offenses. This approach is based on the belief that harsh penalties serve as a deterrent to criminal behavior.

Project 2025 also proposes to restrict the discretion of prosecutors, particularly in offering plea deals or reducing charges for offenders. The project argues that too much leniency in prosecutorial decisions can lead to reduced accountability for criminal behavior. By imposing stricter guidelines, the project aims to ensure that offenders receive the full extent of legal penalties.

Emphasis on Law and Order

A central component of Project 2025's criminal justice policies is an emphasis on increasing policing and surveillance to maintain law and order. This includes expanding police forces, increasing funding for law enforcement agencies, and implementing advanced surveillance technologies. The project argues that a robust law enforcement presence is essential for deterring crime and ensuring public safety.

Project 2025 advocates for tough-on-crime legislation that imposes severe penalties for a wide range of offenses. This includes not only violent crimes but also property crimes and drug offenses. The project supports policies that prioritize incarceration over rehabilitation, based on the belief that stringent punishment is necessary to maintain societal order.

To accommodate the expected increase in incarceration rates resulting from tougher sentencing laws, Project 2025 calls for the expansion of prison infrastructure. This includes building new facilities and upgrading existing ones to ensure they can handle higher inmate populations. The project also supports private prison partnerships to manage the increased demand.

While rehabilitation programs have gained traction as a means to reduce recidivism and support offender reintegration into society, Project 2025 de-emphasizes these initiatives. The project views rehabilitation as secondary to punishment and deterrence, arguing that the primary goal of the criminal justice system should be to incapacitate offenders and protect the public.

Project 2025 places a strong emphasis on protecting the rights of crime victims. This includes advocating for policies that ensure victims receive restitution and have a voice in the criminal justice process. The project argues that prioritizing victim rights helps restore public confidence in the justice system and ensures that justice is served.

This approach to criminal justice represents a significant shift away from recent reform efforts. By opposing progressive policies and emphasizing law and order, the project seeks to implement a more punitive and traditional model of criminal justice. Project 2025 prioritizes strict punishment, increased policing, and the expansion of prison infrastructure over rehabilitation and systemic reform, which will have a significant impact on society at large.

Impact on Marginalized Communities

The criminal justice policies proposed by Project 2025, with their focus on rolling back reforms and emphasizing law and order, are likely to have profound and detrimental effects on marginalized communities.

Here's a closer look at how these policies might impact these groups:

Increased Incarceration Rates: Marginalized communities, particularly Black and Hispanic populations, have historically been disproportionately affected by punitive criminal justice policies. The reinstatement of mandatory minimum sentences and the rollback of reforms aimed at reducing incarceration rates are expected to lead to a surge in the number of people from these communities being imprisoned. This exacerbates existing disparities and further entangles individuals and families in the criminal justice system.

Economic Consequences: Higher incarceration rates among marginalized communities lead to significant economic disadvantages. Incarceration disrupts employment, reduces earning potential, and imposes financial burdens on families through legal fees, lost income, and the costs associated with maintaining contact with incarcerated loved ones. These economic strains can perpetuate cycles of poverty and limit opportunities for upward mobility.

Erosion of Trust in Law Enforcement: The increased policing and surveillance proposed by Project 2025 are likely to strain relationships between law enforcement and marginalized communities. Historically, these communities have experienced over-policing and discriminatory practices, leading to mistrust and fear of law enforcement. Enhanced policing efforts without corresponding reforms to address systemic biases could deepen this mistrust and hinder community cooperation with law enforcement.

Reduced Access to Rehabilitation and Support Services: The de-emphasis on rehabilitation programs under Project 2025 means that individuals from marginalized communities will have fewer opportunities for treatment, education, and reentry support. Rehabilitation programs are crucial for reducing recidivism and helping individuals reintegrate into society. Without access to these services, formerly incarcerated individuals may struggle to rebuild their lives, increasing the likelihood of reoffending.

Disproportionate Impact of Tough-on-Crime Legislation: Tough-on-crime laws tend to disproportionately impact marginalized communities due to systemic biases in the criminal justice system. Higher arrest rates, longer sentences, and fewer opportunities for plea bargains can lead to harsher outcomes for people of color. This perpetuates a cycle of inequality and reinforces structural barriers to justice and fairness.

Strain on Community Resources: Communities with high rates of incarceration face additional challenges as resources are diverted from essential services to support the criminal justice system. This can lead to underfunded schools, inadequate healthcare, and insufficient social services, further disadvantaging marginalized communities. The expansion of prison infrastructure proposed by Project 2025 could divert even more resources away from community development and support.

Psychological and Social Impacts: The pervasive presence of law enforcement and the threat of incarceration can have profound psychological effects on individuals and communities. The stress and trauma associated with over-policing, family separation due to incarceration, and the stigmatization of having a criminal record can lead to long-term mental health issues and weaken the social fabric of communities.

Civil Rights Concerns: The emphasis on law and order at the expense of civil rights protections raises significant concerns for marginalized communities. Policies that limit prosecutorial discretion, reduce avenues for challenging discriminatory practices, and prioritize punitive measures over fair treatment can erode the civil rights of individuals from these communities. This undermines efforts to achieve justice and equality within the criminal justice system.

Overall, criminal justice policies proposed by Project 2025 are likely to have severe and far-reaching impacts on marginalized communities. By increasing incarceration rates, reducing access to support services, and reinforcing systemic biases, these policies risk perpetuating cycles of disadvantage and inequality.

Historical Context of Mass Incarceration and Reform Movements

Understanding the historical context of mass incarceration and the subsequent reform movements provides crucial insights into the potential impacts of Project 2025's criminal justice policies. Here's a look at how mass incarceration developed and the efforts to reform the system.

The Rise of Mass Incarceration

War on Drugs

The mass incarceration crisis in the United States began in earnest during the 1970s and 1980s with the War on Drugs. Initiated by President Richard Nixon and escalated under President Ronald Reagan, this campaign aimed to combat drug use and trafficking through stringent law enforcement measures. Policies such as mandatory minimum sentences for drug offenses and the increased use of incarceration for nonviolent drug crimes led to a dramatic rise in the prison population.

Mandatory Minimum Sentences and Three Strikes Laws

Legislation like the Anti-Drug Abuse Act of 1986 introduced mandatory minimum sentences, which removed judicial discretion and imposed severe penalties for drug offenses. The "three strikes" laws, which mandated life sentences for individuals convicted of three serious crimes, further contributed to the growth of the prison population. These policies disproportionately affected communities of color and low-income individuals, exacerbating racial and socioeconomic disparities in the criminal justice system.

Privatization of Prisons

The expansion of private prisons in the 1980s and 1990s also played a role in the rise of mass incarceration. For-profit prison companies lobbied for tougher sentencing laws to ensure a steady stream of inmates, creating financial incentives to maintain high incarceration rates. This shift towards privatization led to concerns about the ethical implications and effectiveness of profit-driven correctional facilities.

Consequences of Mass Incarceration

Social and Economic Impact

The mass incarceration policies resulted in significant social and economic consequences. Millions of individuals, particularly from marginalized communities, were incarcerated, disrupting families and communities. The economic burden of supporting a large prison population strained state and federal budgets, diverting funds from education, healthcare, and social services.

Impact on Racial Disparities

Mass incarceration disproportionately impacted Black and Hispanic communities, leading to stark racial disparities in the criminal justice system. These communities faced higher rates of arrest, conviction, and longer sentences compared to their white counterparts. The systemic biases that contributed to these disparities prompted calls for reform to address racial injustice.

The Emergence of Reform Movements

Early Reform Efforts

In the late 20th and early 21st centuries, awareness of the negative consequences of mass incarceration began to grow. Early reform efforts focused on reducing the use of incarceration for nonviolent offenses, advocating for alternatives such as drug courts, probation, and community service.

The Sentencing Reform and Corrections Act

One significant legislative effort was the Sentencing Reform and Corrections Act, which aimed to reduce mandatory minimum sentences for nonviolent drug offenses and promote rehabilitation programs. Although not passed in its original form, it reflected a growing bipartisan consensus on the need for criminal justice reform.

The First Step Act

In 2018, the First Step Act was signed into law, marking a significant milestone in the criminal justice reform movement. The Act included provisions to reduce mandatory minimum sentences, allow more judicial discretion, and expand early release programs for federal inmates. It also aimed to improve prison conditions and support reentry efforts to reduce recidivism.

Grassroots and Advocacy Movements

Black Lives Matter

The Black Lives Matter movement has been instrumental in highlighting the intersection of racial injustice and criminal justice policies. Protests and advocacy efforts have brought national attention to issues such as police brutality, racial profiling, and the need for comprehensive reform.

Decarceration and Reentry Programs

Grassroots organizations and advocacy groups have championed decarceration efforts, pushing for the release of nonviolent offenders and the implementation of reentry programs. These initiatives focus on providing support for formerly incarcerated individuals to reintegrate into society, find employment, and access education and healthcare.

Current Trends and Challenges

State-Level Reforms

Several states have undertaken significant reforms to address mass incarceration. These include revising sentencing laws, decriminalizing certain offenses, and investing in rehabilitation and diversion programs. States like California, New York, and Texas have made strides in reducing their prison populations and addressing systemic issues within their criminal justice systems.

Ongoing Challenges

Despite progress, challenges remain. Racial disparities persist, and the criminal justice system continues to face scrutiny over practices such as solitary confinement, cash bail, and the treatment of juvenile offenders. Reform advocates emphasize the need for continued efforts to address these issues comprehensively.

The historical context of mass incarceration and the evolution of reform movements underscore the complexity of the criminal justice system and the significant impact of policies like those proposed by Project 2025. Understanding this history is essential for assessing the potential impact of undoing recent reforms and prioritizing punitive measures over rehabilitation and systemic change.

Chapter 6: Attacks on Free Speech and Democracy

Project 2025 poses significant threats to free speech through its proposals for media suppression, control, and targeting of government critics and whistleblowers. These measures could undermine the foundational democratic principle of freedom of expression and restrict the public's ability to hold the government accountable.

Media Suppression and Control

Project 2025 supports policies that could lead to the consolidation of media ownership, allowing a few large corporations to control a significant portion of the media landscape. This consolidation can limit the diversity of viewpoints presented to the public and reduce the media's ability to operate independently from government influence.

The project proposes increasing regulatory pressures on media outlets that criticize the government. This could include imposing fines, revoking licenses, or using other regulatory mechanisms to stifle dissenting voices. By leveraging regulatory authority, the government could coerce media organizations into self-censorship to avoid punitive actions.

Project 2025's approach may also involve direct censorship of media content deemed unfavorable to the government. This could take the form of restrictions on what can be reported, limits on access to information, or the dissemination of state-sponsored propaganda to shape public opinion. Such measures would severely curtail the media's role as a watchdog and guardian of democracy.

Targeting Government Critics and Whistleblowers

Under Project 2025, policies could be enacted that criminalize dissent against the government. This might include expanding laws related to sedition, treason, or incitement to silence critics and activists. Individuals who publicly oppose government policies or actions could face legal repercussions, including arrest and imprisonment.

The project supports increased surveillance of government critics and whistleblowers. This could involve monitoring communications, tracking activities, and using intelligence agencies to gather information on individuals or groups perceived as threats. The aim would be to intimidate and deter individuals from speaking out against the government.

Project 2025 could undermine existing protections for whistleblowers who expose government wrongdoing. This might include repealing or weakening whistleblower protection laws, making it easier for the government to retaliate against individuals who leak information or report misconduct. Retaliatory actions could include job termination, legal action, or other forms of harassment and intimidation.

Legal safeguards that protect free speech, such as the First Amendment and court precedents supporting press freedom, could be eroded under Project 2025. The project might push for judicial appointments that favor restrictive interpretations of free speech rights or advocate for legislative changes that limit these protections. This erosion would weaken the legal framework that supports a free and independent press.

Project 2025's threats to free speech through media suppression, control, and targeting of government critics and whistleblowers pose serious risks to democratic governance. These measures could stifle dissent, reduce transparency, and undermine the public's ability to hold the government accountable.

Implications for Democratic Discourse and Transparency

The threats posed by Project 2025 to free speech and press freedom could have severe implications for democratic discourse and transparency. Here's how these potential changes could affect the democratic fabric of society:

Diminished Public Debate

Free speech and a free press are essential for vibrant public debate. Project 2025's efforts to suppress dissent and control media could stifle the exchange of diverse viewpoints, leading to a more homogenized and less critical public discourse. When only government-approved narratives are allowed to flourish, citizens are deprived of the information and perspectives necessary to make informed decisions.

Erosion of Government Accountability

Transparency in government actions is crucial for holding public officials accountable. By targeting critics and whistleblowers, Project 2025 could create a climate of fear that discourages individuals from exposing wrongdoing. Without whistleblowers and a free press to investigate and report on government activities, instances of corruption, abuse of power, and inefficiency may go unchecked, eroding public trust in institutions.

Weakening of Investigative Journalism

Investigative journalism plays a critical role in uncovering truths that those in power might prefer to keep hidden. The increased regulatory pressures and potential censorship advocated by Project 2025 could hamper journalists' ability to conduct thorough investigations. This weakening of investigative journalism would leave the public less informed and more vulnerable to manipulation by those in power.

Increased Public Mistrust

Suppressing free speech and controlling the media can lead to widespread public mistrust. When citizens believe that information is being manipulated or withheld by the government, confidence in public institutions declines. This mistrust can foster cynicism, disengagement, and polarization, weakening the democratic process and societal cohesion.

Suppression of Activism and Advocacy

A healthy democracy depends on active participation from its citizens, including through activism and advocacy. By criminalizing dissent and intimidating critics, Project 2025 could deter individuals and organizations from engaging in advocacy efforts. This suppression stifles grassroots movements and reduces the diversity of voices in the public sphere, making it harder to challenge unjust policies and advocate for change.

Impact on Policy Development

Open discourse and transparency are crucial for effective policy development. When diverse perspectives are shared and debated, policymakers can make more informed decisions that reflect the needs and concerns of the public. Project 2025's restrictions on free speech could limit these perspectives, leading to policies that may not adequately address the complexities of societal issues.

Undermining Democratic Values

At its core, democracy values the rights of individuals to express their opinions and seek the truth. By attacking these fundamental rights, Project 2025 undermines the very principles that support a democratic society. This shift towards authoritarian control can erode democratic values and weaken the societal fabric that upholds freedom and justice.

Global Implications

The actions taken under Project 2025 could also have global repercussions. As a leading democratic nation, the United States sets an example for other countries. Suppressing free speech and limiting transparency domestically could embolden authoritarian regimes worldwide to adopt similar measures, weakening the global commitment to democratic principles.

Project 2025's threats to free speech and press freedom could profoundly undermine democratic discourse and transparency. These measures risk stifling public debate, reducing government accountability, weakening investigative journalism, and increasing public mistrust.

Strategies for Protecting Free Speech and Press Freedom

In response to the threats posed by Project 2025 to free speech and press freedom, it is essential to adopt strategies that safeguard these fundamental democratic principles. Here are some effective strategies for protecting free speech and ensuring a free and independent press:

Strengthening Legal Protections

- **Enforcing Constitutional Rights:** Robustly defending the First Amendment, which guarantees freedom of speech and the press, is crucial. Legal challenges can be brought against policies that infringe upon these rights, ensuring that they are upheld in courts.

- **Expanding Whistleblower Protections:** Strengthening laws that protect whistleblowers from retaliation can encourage individuals to expose government wrongdoing without fear of reprisal. This helps maintain transparency and accountability.

- **Support for Journalistic Shield Laws:** Advocating for stronger shield laws that protect journalists from being compelled to reveal their sources can preserve the confidentiality necessary for investigative reporting.

Promoting Media Independence

- **Limiting Media Consolidation:** Implementing regulations to prevent excessive consolidation of media ownership can ensure a diverse and independent media landscape. Policies that promote competition and prevent monopolies can help maintain a plurality of voices in the media.

- **Supporting Public Broadcasting:** Investing in public broadcasting services can provide a reliable source of independent news and information free from corporate or political influence. Public broadcasters can serve as a counterbalance to private media companies.

Enhancing Transparency and Accountability

- **Freedom of Information Laws:** Strengthening and enforcing freedom of information laws can ensure that government actions are transparent and accessible to the public. These laws provide journalists and citizens with the tools to hold the government accountable.

- **Independent Oversight Bodies:** Establishing independent oversight bodies, such as press councils or ombudsmen, can monitor media practices and address issues of bias, misinformation, and unethical behavior. These bodies can help maintain journalistic standards and integrity.

Fostering a Culture of Free Expression

- **Education and Public Awareness:** Promoting media literacy and public awareness about the importance of free speech and a free press can empower citizens to advocate for their rights. Educational programs can teach individuals how to critically evaluate information and recognize attempts to suppress free expression.

- **Encouraging Civic Engagement:** Encouraging active participation in democratic processes, such as voting, public protests, and community organizing, can help protect free speech and press freedom. Civic engagement fosters a culture of accountability and resistance to authoritarian measures.

Supporting Journalistic Efforts

- **Funding Investigative Journalism:** Providing grants and financial support for investigative journalism can help reporters pursue in-depth stories that hold power accountable. Philanthropic organizations, non-profits, and crowdfunding can play a significant role in funding independent journalism.

- **Protecting Journalists' Safety:** Implementing measures to ensure the physical and digital safety of journalists is essential. This includes providing training on digital security, offering legal support, and addressing threats and harassment against reporters.

Building Alliances and Coalitions

- **Collaborating with Civil Society Organizations:** Forming alliances with civil society organizations, human rights groups, and advocacy organizations can amplify efforts to protect free speech and press freedom. These coalitions can provide resources, support, and a unified voice in the fight against censorship and suppression.

- **International Solidarity:** Engaging with international organizations, such as the United Nations, the Organization for Security and Co-operation in Europe (OSCE), and the International Press Institute (IPI), can bring global attention to threats against free speech and press freedom. International solidarity can apply pressure on governments to respect and uphold these rights.

Utilizing Technology and Innovation

- **Supporting Digital Platforms:** Encouraging the development and use of digital platforms that promote free expression and independent journalism can counteract attempts at media suppression. Open-source tools, encrypted communication, and decentralized platforms can provide alternative avenues for sharing information.

- **Fighting Censorship Technology:** Employing technology to circumvent censorship, such as virtual private networks (VPNs), Tor networks, and other anonymizing tools, can help individuals access and share information freely.

Protecting free speech and press freedom in the face of Project 2025's threats requires a multifaceted approach. Strengthening legal protections, promoting media independence, enhancing transparency and accountability, fostering a culture of free expression, supporting journalistic efforts, building alliances, and utilizing technology are all crucial strategies. By adopting these measures, society can safeguard the democratic principles of free speech and a free press, ensuring that the government remains accountable and that citizens are well-informed.

Chapter 7: Economic and Social Implications

Project 2025's economic policies are grounded in principles of deregulation and a strong emphasis on free-market economics. These policies aim to reduce government intervention in the economy, promote business growth, and encourage private sector solutions to social and economic issues. However, these approaches carry significant implications for social safety nets and welfare programs.

Deregulation and Free-Market Emphasis

Reducing Regulatory Burdens

Project 2025 advocates for significant deregulation across various sectors of the economy. The goal is to eliminate what it sees as burdensome regulations that stifle business innovation and economic growth. This includes rolling back environmental protections, labor laws, consumer safeguards, and financial regulations. Proponents argue that reducing these regulations will lower costs for businesses, increase competitiveness, and spur job creation and investment.

Encouraging Private Sector Solutions

The project promotes the idea that the private sector is better equipped than the government to address many economic and social issues. By reducing government involvement, Project 2025 seeks to create a more dynamic and efficient economy driven by market forces. This includes privatizing certain public services and encouraging private investment in infrastructure, education, and healthcare.

Tax Cuts and Incentives

Another key component of Project 2025's economic strategy is implementing tax cuts and incentives to stimulate economic activity. This includes lowering corporate tax rates, reducing capital gains taxes, and providing tax breaks for businesses that invest in job creation and innovation. The aim is to create a more favorable business environment that attracts investment and drives economic growth.

Impacts on Social Safety Nets and Welfare Programs

Reduction in Social Safety Nets

One of the most significant implications of Project 2025's economic policies is the potential reduction in social safety nets. By prioritizing deregulation and tax cuts, the project could lead to decreased funding for welfare programs such as unemployment benefits, food assistance, housing subsidies, and healthcare for low-income individuals. These cuts could increase economic insecurity and poverty among the most vulnerable populations.

Shift to Privatized Welfare Solutions

Project 2025 encourages the privatization of many services traditionally provided by the government, including elements of social welfare. This shift assumes that private entities can deliver these services more efficiently and cost-effectively. However, there is concern that privatization may lead to reduced access and quality of services for those who cannot afford to pay, exacerbating inequality.

Impact on Healthcare Access

Reducing regulations and shifting to a more market-driven healthcare system could impact access to care. Deregulation might result in fewer protections for patients and higher costs, making it more difficult for low-income individuals to access necessary medical services. Additionally, cuts to programs like Medicaid could leave millions without affordable healthcare options.

Education and Workforce Development

Deregulation and privatization in education could lead to increased disparities in educational quality and access. Project 2025's policies might prioritize funding for private schools and charter schools over public education, potentially leading to a decline in resources for public schools. This could widen the education gap between wealthy and low-income students, affecting long-term economic mobility and workforce development.

Economic Inequality

The emphasis on free-market policies and deregulation is likely to exacerbate economic inequality. While these policies may benefit businesses and higher-income individuals through tax cuts and reduced regulations, they could increase the economic burden on lower-income populations. The reduction in social safety nets and welfare programs would likely leave many without adequate support.

Community and Social Stability

The reduction in welfare programs and increased economic inequality could lead to greater social instability. Communities that rely heavily on government assistance might experience higher levels of poverty, homelessness, and crime. The resulting social strain could undermine community cohesion and increase tensions between different socioeconomic groups.

While Project 2025's economic policies, characterized by deregulation and a strong free-market emphasis, aim to stimulate economic growth and reduce government intervention, these policies also pose significant risks to social safety nets and welfare programs. The potential reduction in support for vulnerable populations, increased economic inequality, and the privatization of essential services could have far-reaching implications for social stability and equity.

Potential Outcomes for Economic Inequality

The economic policies proposed by Project 2025, with their focus on deregulation, tax cuts, and reduced government intervention, are likely to have significant implications for economic inequality. Here are some potential outcomes:

1. **Widening Wealth Gap:** Project 2025's emphasis on tax cuts, particularly those that benefit corporations and high-income individuals, could lead to a widening wealth gap. While these policies might stimulate economic growth and increase wealth for those at the top, they often do not provide proportional benefits to lower-income individuals. As a result, the rich could become richer while the poor see little improvement in their economic situation.

2. **Reduced Social Mobility:** Economic inequality can hinder social mobility, making it harder for individuals from lower-income backgrounds to improve their economic status. With reduced funding for education, healthcare, and social services, opportunities for upward mobility may diminish. This

could lead to a more entrenched class system where individuals' economic prospects are closely tied to their family background.

3. **Decline in Public Services:** Cuts to social safety nets and public services could disproportionately affect low-income communities. As funding for welfare programs, public education, and healthcare is reduced, these communities may experience a decline in the quality and availability of essential services. This could exacerbate existing inequalities and leave vulnerable populations with fewer resources and support systems.

4. **Increased Poverty Rates:** The reduction or elimination of welfare programs such as food assistance, housing subsidies, and unemployment benefits could lead to an increase in poverty rates. Without these safety nets, individuals who lose their jobs or face financial hardship may struggle to meet basic needs, leading to higher levels of poverty and economic insecurity.

5. **Health Disparities:** Economic inequality often translates into health disparities, as lower-income individuals have less access to healthcare and healthy living conditions. With Project 2025's potential cuts to healthcare programs and the privatization of medical services, these disparities could widen. Poor health outcomes can further entrench economic inequality by limiting individuals' ability to work and earn a living.

6. **Educational Inequities:** Education is a critical factor in economic mobility, but Project 2025's focus on privatization and reduced funding for public schools could exacerbate educational inequities. Wealthier families may be able to afford private education or benefit from well-funded charter schools, while low-income students may be left with under-resourced public schools. This disparity in educational quality can perpetuate economic inequality across generations.

7. **Labor Market Impacts:** Deregulation and a free-market approach might lead to job growth, but the benefits of this growth are not always evenly distributed. High-paying jobs may increase for those with advanced skills and education, while low-wage workers might see less benefit and continued job insecurity. Without strong labor protections and support programs, the gap between high- and low-income workers could grow.

8. **Social Unrest and Instability:** Rising economic inequality can lead to social unrest and instability. As the gap between the wealthy and the poor widens, feelings of injustice and disenfranchisement can grow. This can lead to increased social tensions, protests, and a decline in social cohesion. Governments may face greater challenges in maintaining public order and addressing the needs of their populations.

9. **Long-term Economic Growth:** While Project 2025's policies aim to stimulate short-term economic growth, the long-term effects of increased inequality could undermine this goal. High levels of inequality can reduce overall economic growth by limiting consumer spending, reducing human capital development, and increasing social and economic instability. A more equitable distribution of wealth is often associated with more sustainable and inclusive economic growth.

In summary, the potential outcomes of Project 2025's economic policies for economic inequality are concerning. The focus on deregulation, tax cuts, and reduced social safety nets could lead to a widening wealth gap, reduced social mobility, and increased poverty and health disparities. These outcomes could exacerbate social tensions and undermine long-term economic stability and growth.

Effects on Vulnerable Populations

The economic policies proposed by Project 2025, with their focus on deregulation, reduced government intervention, and privatization, could have disproportionate effects on vulnerable populations. These groups, which include low-income families, minorities, elderly individuals, and people with disabilities, are likely to bear the brunt of the negative impacts. Here are some key ways these policies could affect vulnerable populations:

Increased Poverty and Economic Insecurity

With the reduction or elimination of social safety nets such as food assistance, housing subsidies, and unemployment benefits, vulnerable populations may face heightened economic insecurity. Without these critical supports, individuals who experience financial hardship, job loss, or unexpected expenses may struggle to meet their basic needs, leading to higher rates of poverty and homelessness.

Reduced Access to Healthcare

Cuts to healthcare programs, particularly those serving low-income individuals, such as Medicaid, could significantly reduce access to medical care for vulnerable populations. The privatization of healthcare services may lead to higher costs and fewer affordable options, making it difficult for many to receive necessary treatment. This can result in poorer health outcomes, increased mortality rates, and a greater burden on emergency services.

Educational Disparities

Project 2025's emphasis on privatizing education and reducing funding for public schools could exacerbate educational inequities. Vulnerable populations, including low-income and minority students, may find themselves in underfunded and overcrowded public schools with fewer resources and opportunities. This disparity can hinder academic achievement and limit future economic opportunities, perpetuating cycles of poverty.

Employment Challenges

While deregulation may spur job growth, the benefits are unlikely to be evenly distributed. Vulnerable populations, often employed in low-wage or unstable jobs, may see less benefit from economic growth and continue to face job insecurity. Additionally, cuts to job training and employment support programs can make it harder for these individuals to gain the skills needed to secure better-paying jobs.

Housing Instability

Reducing or eliminating housing subsidies and support programs could lead to increased housing instability and homelessness among vulnerable populations. Without these programs, many individuals and families may be unable to afford stable housing, leading to a rise in evictions and the number of unhoused people.

Nutritional Deficiencies

Cuts to food assistance programs like SNAP (Supplemental Nutrition Assistance Program) could lead to higher rates of food insecurity and malnutrition among low-income families. Vulnerable populations, including children and the elderly, are at particular risk of experiencing the negative health impacts associated with inadequate nutrition.

Impact on Seniors and People with Disabilities

Elderly individuals and people with disabilities often rely on a range of social services and supports to live independently and maintain their quality of life. Cuts to programs such as Social Security, disability benefits, and home care services could severely impact their ability to meet daily needs and access necessary care, leading to greater hardship and reduced quality of life.

Disproportionate Effects on Minorities

Minority communities, already facing systemic inequities, could be disproportionately affected by the economic policies of Project 2025. Reduced access to healthcare, education, and social services can exacerbate existing disparities and widen the gap between minority populations and their more affluent counterparts.

Mental Health Strain

The compounded effects of economic insecurity, reduced access to essential services, and increased stress can significantly impact the mental health of vulnerable populations. Anxiety, depression, and other mental health issues may become more prevalent as individuals struggle to cope with the loss of support systems and increased financial pressures.

The economic policies of Project 2025 could have severe and far-reaching effects on vulnerable populations. By reducing social safety nets, privatizing essential services, and emphasizing deregulation, these policies risk increasing poverty, reducing access to healthcare and education, and exacerbating social inequalities. We must advocate for policies that protect and support the most vulnerable members of society.

Chapter 8: Mobilizing Resistance

As Project 2025 proposes significant changes with potentially far-reaching impacts, grassroots organizations, advocacy groups, and various institutions are mobilizing to resist and challenge its initiatives.

Civil rights organizations such as the American Civil Liberties Union (ACLU), NAACP, and Southern Poverty Law Center (SPLC) are actively working to combat the regressive policies proposed by Project 2025. These groups are prepared to file lawsuits to challenge any actions that they perceive as violating constitutional rights or undermining civil liberties. By leveraging their legal expertise, these organizations aim to protect the rights of marginalized communities and maintain the integrity of democratic institutions.

Organizations focused on environmental protection, such as the Sierra Club and Natural Resources Defense Council (NRDC), are gearing up to oppose deregulation efforts that threaten environmental safeguards. Legal challenges are expected to play a key role in preventing the rollback of regulations that protect air quality, water resources, and endangered species. These groups are also mobilizing public support through campaigns and grassroots actions to raise awareness about the environmental risks associated with Project 2025.

Healthcare advocacy groups are preparing to defend access to medical services, particularly for low-income and vulnerable populations. Organizations like Families USA and the Health Care for America Now (HCAN) coalition are ready to challenge any policy changes that would reduce healthcare coverage or affordability. Legal strategies may include challenging the dismantling of Medicaid expansions or protections for pre-existing conditions.

Public and private educational institutions, along with teachers' unions, are poised to resist changes that threaten public education and educational equity. Legal challenges could be mounted against policies that undermine funding for public schools or erode protections for students with disabilities. Advocacy efforts will also focus on highlighting the importance of equitable access to quality education for all students.

Political Mobilization and Public Awareness Campaigns

Grassroots organizations are at the forefront of efforts to resist Project 2025. These groups are organizing rallies, town hall meetings, and community forums to engage and inform the public about the potential impacts of the project. Forming broad-based coalitions of concerned citizens enable these grassroots movements to pressure elected officials to oppose policies that threaten civil rights, social safety nets, and environmental protections.

Public awareness campaigns are crucial for educating the public about Project 2025's implications. Advocacy groups are utilizing social media, traditional media, and public speaking events to disseminate information and mobilize support. Campaigns are focusing on storytelling, highlighting the personal impacts of policy changes on individuals and communities to make the issues more relatable and urgent.

Political advocacy organizations are intensifying their efforts to influence policymakers. Groups like Common Cause and the League of Women Voters are advocating for policies that promote transparency, accountability, and democratic participation. Lobbying efforts are focused on persuading legislators to oppose regressive measures and support initiatives that protect and expand civil rights and social justice.

Efforts to mobilize voters are critical for ensuring that public opposition to Project 2025 is reflected in electoral outcomes. Organizations such as Rock the Vote and the Voter Participation Center are working to register new voters, particularly in marginalized communities, and encourage high voter turnout in local, state, and national elections. They aim to elect representatives who are committed to upholding democratic values and resisting harmful policies.

Building broad coalitions across various advocacy groups is essential for creating a unified front against Project 2025. Collaborative efforts bring together diverse organizations focused on civil rights, environmental protection, healthcare, education, and economic justice. Working together, these coalitions can amplify their impact and coordinate strategies for effective resistance.

Generally speaking, mobilizing resistance to Project 2025 involves a multi-faceted approach that includes legal challenges, grassroots mobilization, public awareness campaigns, political advocacy, and voter engagement. All are working together to protect democratic values, civil rights, and social equity in the face of proposed regressive policies.

Strategies for Protecting Democratic Institutions

In response to the potential threats posed by Project 2025, it is crucial to adopt comprehensive strategies to protect democratic institutions. These strategies involve legal action, civic engagement, policy advocacy, and coalition-building efforts designed to safeguard the principles of democracy and ensure accountability and transparency in government.

Legal Protections and Challenges

- **Constitutional Safeguards:** Upholding and defending the Constitution is fundamental to protecting democratic institutions. Legal challenges should be prepared to contest any actions that undermine constitutional rights or violate the separation of powers. Courts play a critical role in maintaining checks and balances.

- **Judicial Independence:** Ensuring the independence of the judiciary is crucial. Advocacy for fair judicial appointments and opposition to attempts to undermine judicial autonomy can help preserve the judiciary's role as a check on executive and legislative power.

- **Whistleblower Protections:** Strengthening and enforcing whistleblower protections can encourage individuals within government institutions to report misconduct and corruption without fear of retaliation. Legal frameworks that protect whistleblowers are essential for maintaining transparency and accountability.

Civic Engagement and Education

- **Public Awareness Campaigns:** Informing citizens about the importance of democratic institutions and the potential threats posed by Project 2025 is important. Public awareness campaigns can educate people about their rights and the mechanisms in place to protect democracy.

- **Civic Education Programs:** Implementing and supporting civic education programs that teach citizens, especially young people, about the principles of democracy, the functioning of government, and the importance of active participation can build a more informed and engaged electorate.

- **Voter Mobilization:** Encouraging voter registration and participation in elections ensures that public opinion is reflected in government decisions. Organizations should focus on mobilizing underrepresented communities to increase voter turnout and elect representatives committed to democratic values.

Policy Advocacy and Reform

- **Campaign Finance Reform:** Advocating for campaign finance reform can reduce the influence of money in politics and ensure that elected officials are accountable to their constituents rather than special interest groups. Policies that promote transparency in political donations and limit corporate influence are crucial.

- **Election Integrity:** Ensuring the integrity of the electoral process is fundamental to democracy. Advocacy for secure and accessible voting methods, combating voter suppression, and supporting independent election oversight can protect the sanctity of elections.

- **Government Transparency:** Promoting policies that enhance government transparency, such as robust freedom of information laws and open government initiatives, can ensure that citizens have access to information about government actions and decisions.

Coalition-Building and Collaboration

- **Building Broad Coalitions:** Forming alliances with a diverse range of organizations, including civil rights groups, environmental advocates, labor unions, and faith-based organizations, can create a unified front to defend democratic institutions. Collaborative efforts can amplify impact and coordinate strategies.

- **International Solidarity:** Engaging with international organizations and networks that support democratic governance can provide additional resources and support. Global solidarity can apply pressure on governments to adhere to democratic norms and standards.

Media and Communication

- **Supporting Independent Media:** Protecting and promoting independent media outlets is essential for ensuring a free press. Providing financial support, legal protections, and a safe environment for journalists can help maintain a robust fourth estate.

- **Countering Disinformation:** Developing strategies to counter disinformation and propaganda is critical. Fact-checking initiatives, media literacy programs, and transparent communication from credible sources can help mitigate the impact of false information.

Grassroots Mobilization

- **Community Organizing:** Grassroots organizing at the local level can empower communities to advocate for their interests and hold local officials accountable. Building strong, community-based networks can provide a foundation for broader democratic engagement.

- **Protests and Demonstrations:** Peaceful protests and demonstrations can raise awareness and pressure policymakers to respond to public concerns. Organized, nonviolent actions can draw attention to issues and mobilize broader support.

The Role of Citizens in Safeguarding Democracy

Citizens are the most important element when it comes to safeguarding democracy. The active participation, vigilance, and engagement of citizens like you is essential for maintaining democratic institutions, ensuring accountability, and protecting civil liberties. Here are several ways in which citizens can contribute to the defense of democracy:

Active Participation in the Electoral Process

- **Voting:** Voting is one of the most fundamental ways citizens can influence government policies and leadership. By participating in elections, citizens can ensure that their voices are heard and that elected officials are held accountable to the public.

- **Voter Registration Drives:** Encouraging voter registration and turnout, especially among underrepresented groups, helps strengthen democracy by ensuring a diverse and inclusive electorate.

Engagement in Civic Education

- **Staying Informed:** Citizens should make an effort to stay informed about current events, government policies, and political developments. Accessing multiple news sources and engaging in critical thinking can help individuals understand complex issues and make informed decisions.

- **Civic Education Programs:** Participating in and supporting civic education programs can enhance citizens' understanding of democratic principles, the functioning of government, and their rights and responsibilities.

Advocacy and Activism

- **Joining Advocacy Groups:** Becoming involved with advocacy groups and non-governmental organizations (NGOs) that align with one's values can amplify efforts to protect democratic principles. These organizations often have the resources and expertise to influence policy and advocate for change.

- **Organizing and Participating in Protests:** Peaceful protests and demonstrations can draw attention to critical issues and show widespread public support or opposition. Organizing and participating in such actions can pressure policymakers to address concerns.

Holding Elected Officials Accountable

- **Communicating with Representatives:** Citizens should regularly communicate with their elected officials to express their views, concerns, and expectations. Writing letters, making phone calls, and attending town hall meetings are effective ways to engage with representatives.

- **Monitoring Government Actions:** Vigilant monitoring of government actions and policies is crucial. Citizens can use tools like freedom of information requests and public records to keep track of government activities and ensure transparency.

Community Engagement

- **Building Community Networks:** Strong community networks can support local democratic initiatives and provide a platform for collective action. Engaging with neighbors, participating in community meetings, and collaborating on local projects can strengthen communal bonds and foster civic participation.

- **Supporting Local Media:** Local media play a vital role in covering community issues and holding local officials accountable. Supporting independent local journalism through subscriptions and donations can help maintain a vibrant and informed local press.

Promoting Tolerance and Inclusivity

- **Encouraging Diverse Voices:** Promoting and supporting the inclusion of diverse voices in public discourse is essential for a healthy democracy. Citizens can advocate for the representation of marginalized communities and work to ensure that all perspectives are heard and respected.

- **Combating Discrimination and Hate:** Actively opposing discrimination, hate speech, and intolerance helps create a more inclusive and equitable society. Citizens can support anti-discrimination initiatives and participate in programs that promote understanding and solidarity.

Participating in Public Policy and Decision-Making

- **Attending Public Meetings:** Attending city council meetings, school board meetings, and other public forums allows citizens to engage directly with decision-makers and influence local policies.

- **Serving on Boards and Commissions:** Volunteering to serve on advisory boards, commissions, and committees provides opportunities for citizens to contribute to the governance of their communities and ensure that diverse perspectives are considered in decision-making processes.

Supporting Democratic Reforms

- **Campaign Finance Reform:** Advocating for campaign finance reform can reduce the influence of money in politics and ensure that elected officials are more accountable to their constituents.

- **Election Integrity:** Supporting measures to ensure the integrity and accessibility of elections, such as secure voting systems, non-partisan redistricting, and protections against voter suppression, is critical for maintaining trust in the electoral process.

Citizens have a vital role in safeguarding democracy. Through active participation in the electoral process, engagement in civic education, advocacy and activism, holding elected officials accountable, community engagement, promoting tolerance and inclusivity, participating in public policy, and supporting democratic reforms, individuals can contribute to a robust and resilient democratic society. We all must understand and embrace these responsibilities to ensure our democratic institutions remain strong and responsive to the needs of all citizens.

Conclusion

Project 2025 proposes a comprehensive and ambitious overhaul of various facets of American governance, society, and economy. However, its potential impacts raise significant concerns across several domains.

1. **Centralization of Power:** Project 2025 aims to centralize power within the executive branch, which poses a threat to the system of checks and balances that is fundamental to American democracy. By concentrating authority, the project risks undermining the legislative and judicial branches' ability to provide necessary oversight and accountability.

2. **Dismantling of Federal Agencies:** The project includes plans to eliminate or drastically restructure federal agencies, particularly targeting the Department of Education. Such actions could lead to a significant reduction in public services and

support systems, particularly affecting education, environmental protection, and public health.

3. **Civil Rights and Social Justice:** Project 2025's stance on civil rights, including efforts to roll back diversity, equity, and inclusion initiatives, and redefine discrimination, could reverse decades of progress toward racial and gender equality. The reduction in protections and support for marginalized communities could exacerbate existing inequalities and social tensions.

4. **Reproductive Rights:** By imposing severe restrictions on abortion and contraceptives, Project 2025 threatens to undermine women's reproductive rights. This could have profound impacts on women's health, autonomy, and socio-economic status, particularly affecting low-income and minority women.

5. **Criminal Justice:** Project 2025's emphasis on law and order, coupled with opposition to reform efforts, could exacerbate mass incarceration issues and disproportionately impact marginalized communities. By prioritizing punitive measures over rehabilitation, the project risks perpetuating cycles of poverty and disenfranchisement.

6. **Free Speech and Democracy:** The project's proposals to suppress dissent, control the media, and target critics pose serious risks to free speech and press freedom. These actions could undermine democratic discourse, reduce government transparency, and erode public trust in democratic institutions.

7. **Economic and Social Inequality:** The economic policies of Project 2025, focused on deregulation and a free-market approach, could widen economic inequality. The reduction in social safety nets and welfare programs could leave vulnerable

populations without essential support, increasing poverty and social instability.

8. **Mobilizing Resistance:** In response to these threats, various advocacy groups, grassroots organizations, and institutions are mobilizing to resist Project 2025. Legal challenges, public awareness campaigns, and political advocacy are crucial strategies to protect democratic values and civil rights.

9. **Role of Citizens:** Citizens play a vital role in safeguarding democracy. Through active participation in the electoral process, civic engagement, advocacy, and community organizing, individuals can contribute to protecting democratic institutions and ensuring accountability and transparency in government.

The Importance of Vigilance and Action

In light of the potential impacts of Project 2025, it is crucial to emphasize the importance of vigilance and action. Protecting democratic values, civil rights, and social equity requires constant awareness and proactive engagement from all citizens. Without vigilance, the risks of authoritarianism, erosion of civil liberties, and increased inequality can go unchecked, leading to significant and lasting harm to society.

Maintaining Democratic Principles

Vigilance is essential to ensure that democratic principles, such as the rule of law, checks and balances, and the separation of powers, are upheld. By staying informed and actively monitoring government actions, citizens can identify and challenge any attempts to undermine these foundational elements of democracy.

Protecting Civil Rights

Ongoing attention to civil rights issues is necessary to safeguard the progress made in achieving equality and justice. Advocacy for policies that promote diversity, equity, and inclusion, as well as resistance to measures that threaten these values, is vital for maintaining a fair and just society.

Ensuring Transparency and Accountability

Transparency in government actions and accountability of public officials are cornerstones of a healthy democracy. Citizens must demand openness in decision-making processes and hold leaders accountable for their actions. This can be achieved through public advocacy, legal challenges, and active participation in civic life.

Combating Economic Inequality

Addressing economic inequality requires sustained effort and advocacy for policies that provide support and opportunities for all citizens. Vigilance against measures that disproportionately benefit the wealthy at the expense of the vulnerable is crucial for fostering a more equitable society.

It's Time to Engage

In addition to being vigilant, it is imperative for readers to actively engage in democratic processes. Democracy thrives when citizens participate fully and contribute to the collective decision-making that shapes their society. Here are some specific actions you can take:

1. **Vote in every election.** Voting is one of the most direct ways to influence government policies and leadership. Ensure you are registered to vote, stay informed about the candidates and issues, and participate in every local, state, and national election.

2. **Stay informed and educated.** Keep yourself informed about current events, government actions, and policy proposals. Access multiple news sources, engage in critical thinking, and participate in discussions to broaden your understanding of important issues.

3. **Join advocacy groups.** Get involved with organizations that align with your values and work towards causes you care about. These groups can amplify your voice, provide resources and support, and offer opportunities for collective action.

4. **Communicate with elected officials.** Reach out to your representatives at all levels of government to express your views, concerns, and expectations. Effective communication with elected officials can influence their decisions and ensure that they represent your interests.

5. **Participate in community organizing.** Engage with your local community through organizing efforts, attending town hall meetings, and participating in civic organizations. Strong community networks can drive local change and create a foundation for broader societal impact.

6. **Advocate for policy reforms.** Support policy reforms that enhance democratic governance, protect civil rights, and promote social equity. Advocate for changes that address systemic issues and improve the well-being of all citizens.

7. **Support independent media.** Independent journalism ensures that the public stays well-informed. Support local and independent media outlets through subscriptions, donations, and by sharing reliable information.

8. **Stand against injustice.** Whenever you witness injustice or discrimination, take a stand. Whether through peaceful protest, public speaking, or legal action, use your voice and actions to oppose wrongdoing and support those who are marginalized.

As we have seen, Project 2025 is poised to have a tremendous negative impact on the United States and the lives of every citizen—including you. Right now, there is a dire need for vigilance and active engagement from all citizens. By staying informed, participating in democratic processes, and advocating for justice and equality, citizens like you can help protect and strengthen the democratic institutions and values essential for a fair and just society. Your involvement is crucial for ensuring a resilient democracy that serves all of us.

Democracy at Risk

Other Books by J. E. Fowlers:

Supreme Court Gone Rogue: The Trump Immunity Case, Its Context in History & What It Means for Democracy